Being A Bug Scout

by Carol Pugliano-Martin

W9-DGX-155

Table of Contents

Introduction

Some scientists say there are about one quintillion bugs in the world. How many is that? Well, it's about one billion bugs for every person! In other words, it's a bug's world and we're just living in it!

The world of bugs is wonderful and fascinating. The activities in this book are designed to give you a closer look at it. But you must remember that bugs are our neighbors—and we need to be good neighbors. So it's very important that you are kind to the bugs you use in these activities. Treat them gently when you catch and work with them.

You can find bugs outdoors or you can buy them from a pet store or **biological** supply company. On page 30, you will find a list of some of these companies.

Do you recognize any of these bugs?

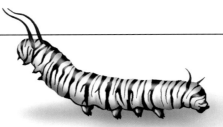

You should keep your bugs for only a short time. When you finish each activity, return your bugs to where you found them. If you bought bugs from a pet store, return them to the store. Do not release these bugs. They may not survive in the wild.

You will need to be careful as you do the activities. Many bugs are good neighbors, but some may bite. Do not touch them directly. You may want to keep a "bug journal" to record your observations as you do the activities.

Now get out there and find some bugs!

What do you get when you cross an insect with a rabbit?

A bug's bunny!

CHAPTER 1

Catch Me If You Can!

You can use different kinds of containers to catch and keep your bugs for a short time. Glass jars, shoe boxes, and plastic containers all work well. It's important to make sure there are air holes punched in the top of whatever container you use.

Different bugs require different materials for their temporary homes. Use the chart on page 5 to gather the required materials for the bugs used in the activities in this book.

You should keep your bugs in their containers for as short a time as possible. If you set up your activity before you catch the bugs, you can minimize the time the bugs are in their temporary homes.

Here's What These Bugs Need	
	**spider** wet cotton ball
	**sow bugs** damp soil, dead leaves
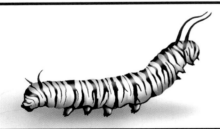	**caterpillar** leaves (the kind on which you found the caterpillar)
	**ants** soil, bread crumbs or graham cracker crumbs

You will be working with the bugs in this chart.
Here's what you'll need for their survival.

See Me Spin!

Perhaps you already know that spiders produce silk. A thread of silk in some spider webs is stronger than a piece of steel the same size! However, not all spiders use silk to build webs.

Spiders that do use silk often weave **intricate** webs. A common type of web is an **orb** web. An orb web is made across an open area. The web that you'll observe being spun in this activity is an orb web.

Spiders spin webs to capture **prey**. When a bug crawls or flies into a spider web, it gets caught in the sticky threads. As the bug moves around, it causes **vibrations** in the threads of the web. The vibrations alert the spider, and it crawls to where the bug remains captured. The spider either eats the bug right away or wraps it in silk to eat later.

an orb weaver spider
in its web

You can observe the fascinating process of a spider spinning a web with this activity.

What you need:

◎ wire coat hanger

◎ wood block, 16 inches long x 4 inches wide x ½ inch thick

◎ wet cotton ball

◎ large, clear plastic bag with twist tie

◎ black-and-yellow garden spider or other kind of spider (see sidebar)

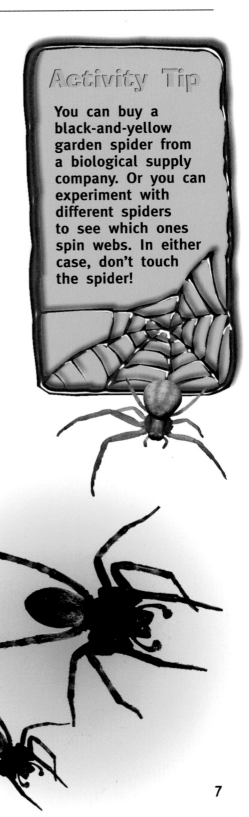

Activity Tip

You can buy a black-and-yellow garden spider from a biological supply company. Or you can experiment with different spiders to see which ones spin webs. In either case, don't touch the spider!

✔ **Point**

Make Connections

Many fiction stories are about spiders. Have you read *Charlotte's Web* or the Anansi stories? Is the information in those stories similar to what you learned here?

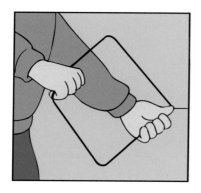

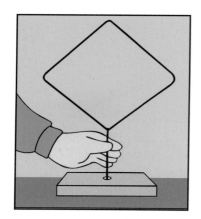

What to do:

1. Ask an adult to help you remove the hooked part of the hanger by bending it back and forth several times.

2. Bend the hanger into a square shape.

3. Ask an adult to help you insert the hanger, sharp side down, into the wood block.

4. **Inflate** the plastic bag and put the hanger and wood block inside it. Place the wet cotton ball on the wood block. The wet cotton ball will keep the air in the bag **moist**. You can inflate the bag by holding the two corners at the open end of the bag and waving it through the air.

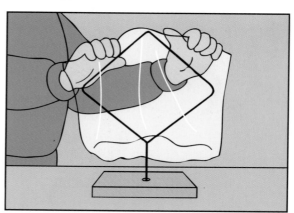

5. Release the spider from its container onto the wood block and quickly seal the plastic bag with a twist tie. **CAUTION: Do not touch the spider**.

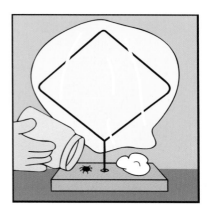

6. Keep the spider in a safe, quiet place where you can watch it, but where it won't be disturbed. Observe the spider for two days. Did it spin a web?

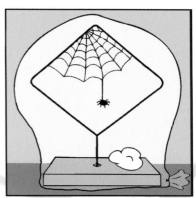

7. If the spider did not spin a web, wait one more day. If there is still no web, release or return that spider and repeat the activity using another kind of spider.

Why did the fly fly?

Because the spider spied her.

CHAPTER 3

Finders Keepers

Spider webs are quite beautiful and unique. No two webs are exactly alike. You may want to preserve nature's beauty.

You can use the web from the activity on page 6 after you release your spider. Or you can find a web on fences, window frames, in basements, and between garden plants and shrubs.

To make sure a spider isn't using the web, tap very gently on the **strands** of silk. If the web is being used, a spider will come running, thinking your tap is a trapped insect. If no spider shows up, it's safe to assume the web is not being used.

What you need:

◎ piece of black construction paper

◎ spray can of white enamel

◎ spray can of clear enamel

◎ scissors

Spider webs are fascinating structures. No two webs are exactly alike.

What to do:

1. Ask an adult to help you spray an unoccupied web on both sides with white enamel. Don't get too close to the web as you spray it or the web will break.

2. While the enamel is wet, mount the web on the black construction paper. This might be more easily done if you hold the construction paper upright. Try to touch all the parts of the web to the paper at the same time.

3. Cut the strands that hold the web to whatever object you found it on.

4. Lay the paper flat so the web can dry.

5. Ask an adult to spray the web with clear enamel.

It's a Fact!

Spiders are not insects. Insects have three body parts; spiders have two. Insects have six legs; spiders have eight. Spiders also do not have **antennae**, wings, and the same kind of eyes as insects.

Which Way Should the Sow Bug Go?

Some people call them sow bugs. Others call them pill bugs. Still others call them roly-polies. But no matter what you call them, these little creatures are fascinating!

Actually, there is a difference between sow bugs and pill bugs. Pill bugs, or roly-polies, can roll up into little balls to protect themselves. Sow bugs stay flat and run under rocks and leaves for protection. In the activity that follows, the materials call for sow bugs. However, you can use either kind of bug.

Sow bugs can be found in dark, moist places such as under rocks, logs, or in a pile of dry leaves. Happy sow bug hunting!

What you need:

- ◎ shoe box

- ◎ scissors

- ◎ strong glue or modeling clay

- ◎ cardboard

- ◎ a source of light such as a flashlight or small lamp

- ◎ 5 to 10 sow bugs in a container filled with damp soil and dead leaves

☑ **Point**

Talk About It

Sow bugs go by many different names. Reread page 12 and identify the various names. Talk to a group member about what you call them.

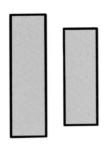

What to do:

1. Cut strips of cardboard to form the walls of a **maze.** You will need two strips: one strip should be 7 inches long and the other one should be 6 inches long. The strips can be 1 to 2 inches wide.

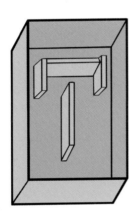

2. Arrange the walls inside the shoe box as follows. Place the 7-inch strip lengthwise in the center. Leave about 1 inch between it and the side of the shoe box. Bend the ends of the 6-inch strip as shown. Place it perpendicular to the other strip, making sure to leave 1 inch between it and the 7-inch strip. Use glue or clay to keep the strips in place.

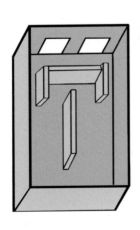

3. Ask an adult to help you cut flaps in the shoe box at each end of the 6-inch strip. You should cut two flaps. Cut the bottom and the two sides so that you can open each flap from the bottom. The sow bugs will exit through those flaps.

4. Remove one sow bug from your container. Place it in the bottom of the T. Once it crawls up the leg of the T, observe which way it turns, to the left or to the right. Open the flap at the bug's chosen exit so it can go out.

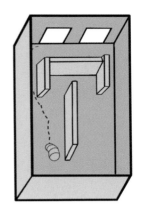

5. Put that sow bug back in the container and repeat step 4 with the rest of the sow bugs. Keep track of how many bugs go to the left and how many go to the right.

6. Next, shine your light source through one opened flap and let the sow bugs go through the maze again. What, if anything, do you notice? Why do you think this happens?

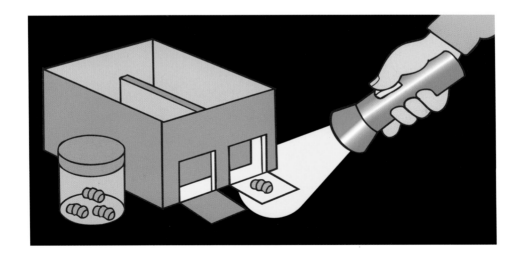

Oh, Give Me a Home!

Mother Nature might be called a magician when one considers the change of a caterpillar into a butterfly or moth. This change is called **metamorphosis.** Here is your chance to watch this amazing process yourself!

You can find caterpillars on top of or under leaves of trees or bushes during the spring. Or you can order them through a biological supply company (see page 30). If you find your caterpillar outside, make sure you take some of the branches and leaves of the tree or bush on which you found it. That is what you will feed the caterpillar in its temporary home.

When your butterfly or moth has emerged from its **chrysalis,** make sure you release it outdoors in the spring or summer only. At that time there are flowers blooming and sources of food for the butterfly or moth.

What you need:

◎ cardboard box, about 18 inches x 12 inches

◎ paper towels

◎ clear plastic wrap

◎ rubber band

◎ tape

◎ scissors

◎ pen or pencil

◎ 10- to 16-ounce plastic or glass jar

◎ water

◎ caterpillar

◎ leaves and branches on which you found the caterpillar or those recommended by a biological supply company if you purchased it.

This caterpillar is enjoying a tasty meal at the end of a tree branch.

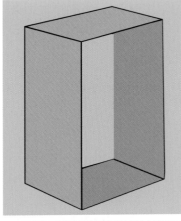

What to do:

1. Cut the bottom and top out of the cardboard box. If the box you are using has flaps, push in the flaps so there are two large, open sides.

2. Turn the box over so the cutout top and bottom are now the front and back of the box.

3. Cut a flap in one side of the box. The flap should be large enough to allow a hand holding supplies to fit through.

4. Poke a few small air holes in the top of the box.

5. Cover the bottom of the box with a damp paper towel. This will keep the box humid. **Humidity** makes it easier for caterpillars to breathe through the tiny holes in the sides of their bodies.

6. Fill the jar half-full with water and cover the opening with plastic wrap. Hold the plastic wrap in place with the rubber band.

7. Poke the stem of the branch on which you found the caterpillar through the plastic into the water. This will keep the branch and leaves from drying out and the caterpillar from falling into the water.

8. Place some leaves on the bottom of the box. Prop a few branches against the cardboard sides. This is where the caterpillar might crawl when it is ready to become a **pupa**.

9. Collect a caterpillar and put it in the box. CAUTION: **Some species of caterpillars have hairs that can cause a nasty skin rash. Try not to handle your caterpillar.**

10. Cover both open sides with clear plastic wrap. Tape the wrap in place so that the box is completely sealed.

11. Keep the box in a warm place that is about the same temperature as the average outdoor temperature, but not in direct sunlight.

12. Add leaves for food as needed. Put a clean, damp paper towel in the bottom of the box daily.

13. Soon after the butterfly or moth has emerged from its chrysalis and its wings have dried, take the box to a flower garden and release the butterfly or moth to nature.

How is a piece of bread like a caterpillar?

They both make the butterfly!

It's a Fact!

Steps of Metamorphosis

Egg – The female butterfly lays her eggs on a leaf.

Caterpillar – The caterpillars hatch within a few days. The caterpillars eat leaves from the plant on which they hatched. They grow fast!

Pupa – After a few weeks, the caterpillars stop eating and enter resting state. Then they will form a hard coverings around themselves. They are now called pupas.

Butterfly – After a few weeks, the hard coverings split open and adult butterflies come out.

Old MacAntie Had a Farm

People who want to learn about living and working together should watch ants and take some tips. Ants live in large groups called **colonies**. Different kinds of ants live in the colony, and each has its own job. The queen is the only ant that lays eggs. She is larger than the other ants. Worker ants take care of the queen. Soldier ants protect the colony. You can observe ants by doing this activity.

To find ants, dig where there is sandy soil. Use a big scooper, such as a shovel, bucket, or large jar, to get a good-sized bunch of ants. Some species of ants bite, so be careful not to touch the ants as you collect them and bring them to their temporary ant farm.

What you need:

- large, wide-mouth glass jar, tank, or bowl

- cheesecloth or other closely woven covering

- large, thick rubber band or string

- black construction paper

- tape

- sand and soil (enough to fill the chosen container almost to the top)

- bread or graham cracker crumbs

- eyedropper

- measuring spoons

- 2 to 3 tablespoons water

- large spoon

- about 30 ants from the same colony

- 1 to 1 ½ tablespoons sugar

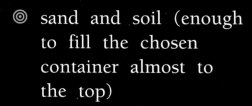

Read More About It

Using reference materials, determine why an ant bite hurts so much.

CHAPTER 6

What to do:

1. Mix together an equal amount of sand and soil. Using the large spoon, put the mixture in the jar, tank, or bowl.

2. Dissolve one tablespoon of sugar in two tablespoons of water. Fill the eyedropper with this liquid. Squirt drops into the sand-soil mixture. Add a handful of graham cracker crumbs or bread crumbs.

3. Carefully place the ants in the container. Remember not to touch them! Cover the mouth of the container with cheesecloth. Keep the cheesecloth in place with the large rubber band or string.

4. Cover the sides and top of the container with the black construction paper, using the tape to secure it to the container.

5. Keep the container in a safe and quiet place.

6. Every day for one week, remove the construction paper on the top and feed the ants sugar and crumbs. Re-cover.

7. After five days, remove the construction paper. Observe the amazing tunnels the ants have made.

8. Release the ants outdoors.

More Ant Antics

If you were to open a restaurant for ants, what types of food would you serve? You can find out what ants like to eat by doing this activity

What you need:

◎ plastic or paper plate

◎ marker

◎ variety of foods—dead leaves, fresh leaves, honey, peanut butter, bread, grass, fruit, or any other foods you can think of

◎ lime juice

◎ diet and regular soda

What to do:

1. Find an ant colony away from your home or school.

2. Mark off the plate into 6 or more sections.

3. Place small, equal amounts of the foods you have chosen to use on the plate, one in each section. Place the plate in a safe location so that no other animals take the food.

4. After several hours, return to see if any ants have found the food. Which food did they take? Which did they leave uneaten? Why do you think they liked some foods more than others?

5. In Central America, people use lime juice to keep ants away from places. After you do the food experiment the first time, try doing it a second time adding some lime juice to foods the ants enjoyed. Does it keep them away?

6. Now see if the size of the food you use changes the ants' feeding behavior. Do they prefer a big piece of bread, crumbled bread, or bread crumbs?

7. After all this eating, the ants may be thirsty! Which do you think they'd prefer to drink—diet soda or regular soda? Set up a taste test and see for yourself. Put a few drops of diet soda on a hard surface, such as a concrete walkway, rock, or patio near some ants. Then put a few drops of the same flavor soda that is sugar-sweetened about six inches away from the diet-soda drops. Do the ants prefer the diet soda or the soda sweetened with sugar?

It's a Fact!

Did you know that ants are one of nature's strongest animals? An ant can lift five times its own weight. For example, if you were as strong as an ant and you weighed 100 pounds, you would be able to lift something that is 500 pounds!

List of Required Materials and Biological Supply Companies

containers for bug-collecting:
  glass jars, shoe boxes, plastic
  containers
water
cotton balls
damp soil
dead leaves
branches/leaves on which you
  find a caterpillar
soil
sand
bread or graham cracker crumbs
wire coat hanger
wood block
  (4 in. x 16 in. x ½ in.)
  clear. plastic bag
  with twist tie
spider (black-and-yellow garden
  spider or other)
spider web
black construction paper
spray can of white enamel
spray can of clear enamel
scissors
cardboard

modeling clay or strong glue
light source – flashlight or
  small lamp
cardboard box (18 in. x 12 in.)
paper towels
clear plastic wrap
tape
small glass jar
caterpillar
large, wide mouth glass jar,
  tank, or bowl
cheesecloth or other
  closely woven covering
large thick rubber band or string
eye dropper
measuring spoons
about 30 ants
large spoon
sugar
plastic or paper plate
marker
different foods for ants:
  honey, peanut butter, bread,
  grass, fruit, etc.

Carolina Biological Supply Company

2700 York Road
Burlington, NC 27215
800-334-5551
www.carolina.com

Connecticut Valley Biological Supply Company, Inc.

82 Valley Road
P.O. Box 326
Southhampton, MA 01073
800-628-7748

GLOSSARY

antennae	(an-TEN-ay) feelers on the head of an insect (page 11)
biological	(BY-oh-LO-Jik-uhl) having to do with the study of living things (page 2)
chrysalis	(KRIS-uh-lis) a butterfly at the stage of development between a caterpillar and an adult butterfly (page 16)
colony	(COHL-uh-nee) large groups of insects that live together (page 22)
humidity	(HYOO-mid-ih-tee) the amount of moisture in the air (page 18)
inflate	(in-FLAYT) to make something larger by blowing or pumping air into it (page 8)
intricate	(IN-trih-ket) finely detailed (page 6)
maze	(MAYZ) a network of paths or lines, made as a puzzle to find your way through (page 14)
metamorphosis	(MET-uh-MORF-uh-sis) the series of changes certain animals go through as they develop from eggs to adults (page 16)
moist	(MOYST) slightly wet (page 8)
orb	(ORB) something that is ball-shaped (page 6)
prey	(PRAY) an animal that is hunted by another animal for food (page 6)
pupa	(POO-pah) an insect at the stage of development between a larva and an adult (page 19)
strand	(STRAND) something that looks like a thread (page 10)
vibration	(VY-bray-shon) fast back-and-forth movement (page 6)

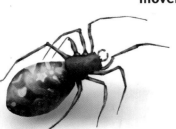

INDEX